THOR & LOKI

IN THE LAND OF GIANTS

A
NORSE
MYTH

STORY BY
JEFF LIMKE

PENCILS AND INKS BY
RON RANDALL

ICELAND

SCANDINAVIA

NORWAY

ATLANTIC
OCEAN

DENMARK

GREAT
BRITAIN

NORTH
SEA

SCANDINAVIA
Lands of the Norse

THOR & LOKI

IN THE LAND OF GIANTS

RUSSIA

FINLAND

SWEDEN

A NORSE MYTH

BALTIC SEA

GRAPHIC UNIVERSE™ • MINNEAPOLIS

THOR AND LOKI ARE TWO OF THE MOST FAMOUS OF THE LEGENDARY GODS OF NORSE MYTHOLOGY. THE STORIES OF THEIR ADVENTURES HAVE BEEN PASSED DOWN THROUGH THE MEDIEVAL WORK THE *PROSE EDDA*. THIS WORK WAS WRITTEN AROUND 1200 BY SNORRI STURLUSON, A POET AND POLITICIAN LIVING IN ICELAND. FOR THIS BOOK, AUTHOR JEFF LIMKE CONSULTED MODERN RETELLINGS OF THOR AND LOKI'S LEGENDARY JOURNEY TO THE LAND OF THE GIANTS, INCLUDING *BULFINCH'S MYTHOLOGY*, THE CLASSIC WORK OF AMERICAN THOMAS BULFINCH. ARTIST RON RANDALL CONSULTED NUMEROUS REFERENCE BOOKS ON MEDIEVAL VIKINGS AS WELL AS ART FROM THE ANCIENT NORSE PERIOD TO BRING TO LIFE THE VIVID IMAGES OF THIS STORY.

STORY BY JEFF LIMKE

PENCILS AND INKS BY RON RANDALL

COLORING BY HI–FI DESIGN

LETTERING BY BILL HAUSER

Graphic Universe™
A division of Lerner Publishing Group, Inc.
241 First Avenue North
Minneapolis, MN 55401 U.S.A.

Website address: www.lernerbooks.com

Library of Congress Cataloging-in-Publication Data

Limke, Jeff.
    Thor and Loki : in the land of giants : a Norse myth / by Jeff Limke ; illustrated by Ron Randall.
        p.   cm. — (Graphic Myths and Legends)
    Includes bibliographical references.
    ISBN-13: 978-0-8225-3087-9 (lib. bdg. : alk. paper)
    ISBN-10: 0-8225-3087-2 (lib. bdg. : alk. paper)
        1. Thor (Norse deity)—Juvenile literature. 2. Loki (Norse deity)—Juvenile literature. I. Randall, Ron. II. Title. III. Series: Graphic myths and legends (Minneapolis, Minn.)
    BL870.T5L56 2007
    398.209363—dc22   2005033069

Manufactured in the United States of America
3 – JR – 1/1/10

TABLE OF CONTENTS

LOKI, MY BROTHER, YOU REALLY DON'T UNDERSTAND.

IN NORSE MYTHOLOGY, TWO GODS ARE VERY POPULAR.

ULTIMATELY, YOU NEED *STRENGTH* BECAUSE IT WILL ALWAYS GET YOU OUT OF WHATEVER TROUBLE YOU ARE IN.

THOR, THE GOD OF THUNDER, WAS STRONG AND CARRIED WITH HIM A MAGIC HAMMER CALLED *MJOLNIR*.

LOKI WAS KNOWN AS THE *TRICKSTER GOD* BECAUSE HE WOULD ALWAYS TRY TO FIND A SNEAKY SOLUTION TO A PROBLEM AND—

NO, THOR, IT DOESN'T *ALWAYS* WORK THAT WAY.

A VISIT FROM THE GODS

HE SOMETIMES USED TRICKS TO OUTWIT BOTH ENEMIES AND FRIENDS.

LOOK, WE HAVE LEFT OUR HOME IN *ASGARD* TO JOURNEY TO *THE LAND OF GIANTS*.

THERE YOU'LL SEE THAT I'M RIGHT. BRAINS WILL ALWAYS BEAT BRAWN.

6

7

9

THE HOME OF THE FROST GIANTS

NOW, BE VERY CAREFUL INSIDE. WATCH WHAT YOU SAY.

UTGARD-LOKI AND THE OTHER GIANTS WILL NOT TAKE KINDLY TO LITTLE ONES LIKE YOU BEING BOASTFUL.

WHO IS HE TO TELL ME NOT TO SPEAK OF MY GRAND DEEDS?

HE'S THE GIANT YOU COULD *BARELY WAKE*, REMEMBER?

VERY FUNNY, VERY FUNNY.

YOU WERE THE ONE WHO ARGUED YOUR STRENGTH COULD HANDLE ANYTHING. IT WASN'T HOW SMART SOMEONE WAS. IT WAS HOW *STRONG*.

I STILL THINK THAT. LOOK AROUND, YOU THINK THESE GIANTS ARE GOING TO RESPECT SOME TRICK YOU PULL ON THEM?

OH, I THINK THEY WOULD RESPECT IT.

I DON'T, AND I'LL END UP HAVING TO PROVE YOU WRONG—

AGAIN.

I'M AFRAID THIS IS AS FAR AS YOU CAN GO.

NO ONE IS ALLOWED INSIDE UNLESS THEY CAN PROVE THEIR STRENGTH.

WHAT DID I SAY?

LOGI WINS!

THIS IS NOT HAPPENING.

YOU BOTH HAVE EMBARRASSED ME.

I WILL DO THE REST OF THESE CHALLENGES.

GLOSSARY AND PRONUNCIATION GUIDE

ASGARD (*az*-gard): the home of the Norse gods

CRONE: an old woman

LEMMINGS: small, short-tailed, furry-footed rodents that live in northern regions

LOKI (*loh*-kee): the trickster in Norse mythology, often identified as Thor's brother

MIDGARD SERPENT: a giant serpent that circles the earth, according to Norse legend

MJOLNIR (my-uhl-*neer*): Thor's magic hammer

MORTAL: a being that dies

ODIN (*oh*-din): father of the Norse gods

THOR: the Norse god of Thunder

UTGARD–LOKI (*oot*-gard *loh*-kee): king of the Norse giants

pencil from page 32

FURTHER READING AND WEBSITES

Philip, Neil. *The Illustrated Book of Myths: Tales and Legends of the World.* New York: Dorling Kindersley, 1995. This illustrated book recounts myths from around the world, including Norse myths.

_____. *Mythology.* New York: Dorling Kindersley, 1999. This volume in the Eyewitness Books series uses dozens of colorful photos and illustrations to explore myths from around the world.

Roberts, Morgan J. *Norse Gods and Heroes.* New York: Metro Books, 1995. Filled with illustrations and photos of ancient mythological artifacts, this book provides an excellent overview of Norse mythology.

Encyclopedia Mythica: Norse Mythology
http://www.pantheon.org/areas/mythology/europe/norse/articles.html
  This helpful website features brief profiles of all of the Norse gods as well as information about many other characters in Norse mythology.

Thomas Bulfinch: Bulfinch's Mythology
http://www.classicreader.com/booktoc.php/sid.2/bookid.2823/
  This website features one of the most popular English-language compilations of ancient myths. This classic work, which includes some Norse myths, was compiled by American Thomas Bulfinch in the 1800s.

CREATING *THOR AND LOKI: IN THE LAND OF GIANTS*

To create the story of Thor and Loki's journey to the land of giants, author Jeff Limke relied heavily on the classic book *Bulfinch's Mythology* by American Thomas Bulfinch. This work drew its material from the *Prose Edda*, a compilation of Norse tales compiled by Icelandic poet and lawyer Snorri Sturluson. Artist Ron Randall consulted numerous reference books on the medieval Vikings as well as art from the ancient Norse period to bring to life the vivid images of this story.

INDEX

ABOUT THE AUTHOR AND THE ARTIST

JEFF LIMKE was raised in North Dakota. There he read, listened to, and marveled at stories from the day he learned to read. He later taught stories for many years, and he has written adaptations of them. Some of his stories have been published by Caliber Comics, Arrow Comics, and Kenzer and Company. Along the way he got married, and he and his wife had a daughter who loves to read, listen to, and marvel at stories.

RON RANDALL has drawn comics for every major comic publisher in the United States, including Marvel, DC, Image and Dark Horse. He has worked on super hero comics such as *Justice League* and *Spiderman*, science fiction titles such as *Star Wars*, *Star Trek* and his own creation *Trekker*, fantasy adventure titles such as *DragonLance* and *Warlord*, and suspense and horror titles including *SwampThing*, *Predator*, and *Venom*. He lives in Portland, Oregon.